Richard Austin's
DOGS & PUPPIES

HALSGROVE

First published in Great Britain in 2005

British Library Cataloguing-in-Publication Data
A CIP record for this title is available from the British Library

ISBN 1 84114 485 1

HALSGROVE
Halsgrove House
Lower Moor Way
Tiverton, Devon EX16 6SS
Tel: 01884 243242
Fax: 01884 243325
email: sales@halsgrove.com
website: www.halsgrove.com
see also: www.richardaustinimages.com

Printed and bound by D'Auria Industrie Grafiche Spa, Italy

Foreword

It was a forebear, Samuel Butler, who made the observation 'The greatest pleasure of owning a dog is that you may make a fool of yourself with him and he will not look down on you, but he will make a fool of himself too...'. And which of us would not own up to enjoying such a moment with their favourite canine.

In this book of 'Animal Magic' photographs Richard Austin captures the essence of why it is we just can't help falling in love with dogs. With each year Richard's reputation as a photographer grows, and along with it comes awards and acclaim both for his work as a press photographer and for his photographs of animals, domestic and wild.

Richard's *Dogs & Puppies* includes his personal selection of wonderful images. From the haughtiest of hounds to the merest of mutts, we can see in each picture something that captivates us, and reminds us of happy times we have spent in the company of 'man's best friend'.

Simon Butler FRSA
The Publisher – Halsgrove

Lucy the Dachshund, who likes to chase the birds from the bird table,
stands guard in case they come back.

Introduction

They say that a dog is man's best friend and who am I to disagree.

Over the years I feel privileged to have come face to face
with a multitude of different breeds of all ages from
newborn pups to those of a more pensionable age.

From working farm dogs, hunting dogs to loveable pets,
I have photographed most of them and have had a
great deal of enjoyment in doing so.

This book is a selection of some of the canine characters
I have encountered along the way.

Richard Austin

Acknowledgements

From a Great Dane to a Jack Russell to wolves and prairie dogs, our canine friends have evolved into a multitude of different species the world over, and man has been associated with them for thousands of years.

This book is just a snapshot of the dogs and pups I have encountered along the way as a newspaper photographer.

Dogs are everyone's best friends, this is the one thing that shines through on the numerous occasions that I, as a photographer, have had the pleasure in coming face to face with the world's most popular pet – the dog.

Keeping the sun off their backs – Archie and Louis the Bulldogs cooling off on a pavement.

Spaniel pups hanging out and the little Pomeranian
dog that vets think is a hermaphrodite.

Sherman the terrier from Tiverton who loves to watch animal programmes on the television.

Mum, Tay, licks her pups clean.

Spaniel pups fast asleep after a feed,
whilst hound pups face an
uncertain future.

Jessie the Border Collie is a favourite with travellers on the
Grand Western Canal at Tiverton in Devon as he
hitches a ride on the barge horse.

For his day job Jim the shire horse tows the barges along the Grand Western Canal at Tiverton. Here he's pictured with his working friends Megan and Jessie 'on top', whilst Winnie prefers life on the ground – with owner Ray Brind.

Border Collies Jessie and Megan hitch a ride on the banks of the Grand Western Canal in Tiverton.

Walkies… Jim and Jessie decide to go for a walk
– with Jessie taking the lead role.

15

Bertie the Retriever is trained to
dive into the water and retrieve the
fish once it has been hooked.

These pups that are pestering mum for milk look more than satisfied once they have been fed.

Monty the Lurcher leaps across a stream on Dartmoor,
whilst (left) the pitiful sight of a washed-up greyhound-
racing dog dumped on the North Devon
Link Road and left to its fate.

Somerset Staghounds keeping their noses in the air.

Wizzer the Dalmatian mum struggles to keep all her pups fed at the milk bar.

Wizzer enjoys her pups' company on the lawn.

Westhighland terrier Chewy and the kitten getting to know each other at the Blue Cross kennels in Bickleigh.

Murray the old softie dog from Secret World Animal Rescue in Somerset. Murray has been a friend and companion to dozens of wild animals looked after at the centre near Highbridge.

A potential Guide Dog for the Blind pup called Hunter plays in the autumn leaves as (right) the spaniel keeps the rain off his head.

King Charles Spaniel with his owner, and
Simba the Afghan racing dog tearing
around the track in Glastonbury.

Carrie the clumsy
Springer spaniel who
injured himself falling
off a wall, although
it didn't stop him
running along the
seafront at Lyme Regis.

Jester makes it the hardest job in the world to clean a dog's teeth when he keeps licking the paste off the brush before it gets in his mouth, and the Shih-tzu called Lady getting ready for the judges.

Almost too many
Corgi puppies to count
as they cram into
their basket.

28

Hounds eager to keep an eye on the proceedings from inside their box.

Roy the Collie sheepdog that injured his back chasing low flying jets over the farmyard.

Roy waits for the RAF.

Corgi puppy in
the flowerbed.

The Morris Dancer's dog with his very own hat, and another dog entered into the Easter bonnet parade.

Japanese Spitz pup safe and sound in a welly boot.

Japanese Spitz pups playing with the welly boots on the lawn.

Why the Border Collie liked to sit in a cement mixer is anybody's guess, but the Yorkshire terrier pup looks cute in the hiking boot.

Best of friends, Fallon the Great Dane and Niamh the terrier enjoy each other's company despite the difference in size.

Lucy the Dachshund pup in the woods, whilst a first outing on a lead for the terrier pup went very well.

Right: The three wrinklies: Shar-Pei Chinese puppies have a lot of skin to grow in to.

Rex the Springer Spaniel on a farmer's demo.

Gismo on the picket line at Devon County Hall.

Animal sanctuaries throw all sorts of animal together, the Alsatian and the kitten seemed to get along just fine. But a nervous truce exsists between Flossie the kitten and skip the terrier pup as the paw of friendship is outstretched

Completely as ease with each other. Rose the Victorian Bulldog and a
homeless kitten called Tish at the Cat Protection HQ near Exeter.

Hound pups stretching up for a better view of the situation.

Hunting hounds have a look of determination as they wait for the huntsman's horn.

The falconer's dramatic end to his display at a country fair was the Harris Hawk landing on the Great Dane. And (below) a stand off of the cockerel and the Golden Labrador pup.

Right: It's a dog's life for the Yorkshire terrier as the Indian Runner ducklings climb all over him.

Not a very polite thing for a dog to do.

A pair of English Bull Terriers.

When the cows are around, it is best to keep out of the way.

Left: Three highly trained Alsation Dogs – Merlin, Rocky and Nuki.

Spot keeps an eye on the lambs at Pennywell Farm in Buckfastleigh.

Above: Skip the sheepdog waiting for his master's whistle.

Right: It takes a lot of concentration to keep sheep under control!

Rounding up the sheep, a sheepdog at work.

Four sheepdogs in training waiting their turn.

Police dogs in training.

Left and below: A study of dogs looking through the railings.

Above: Hounds peep through the gap in the gate.

Midget and Tess at the ready; Springer Spaniels waiting for their master's command.

An army officer takes Otto his Dalmatian for a run on the beach in North Devon.

Russell the pup gets the once-over from racehorse Some Might Say.

A rare sight indeed, a newborn mule foal meets the family
Springer for the first time, and a lucky terrier escapes
a kick from the frisky Shetland pony.

Little dogs with a message: Sparkle declaring
what he likes to hunt and the other lets
everyone know he's on a strict diet.

Some dogs just love the water and making a big splash especially Nipper.

Pampered dogs Kelly and Gemma in the health spa swimming with lifejackets.

The Yorkshire terrier called Hoover with rheumatism enjoys a swim in the health spa.

Right: Yorkshire Terrier Hoover all wrapped up after his swim.

Hound puppies with an uncertain
future since the change in the
law on hunting with dogs.

Rosie the Victorian Bulldog
has a lovely temper
really, even though she
looks like she's waiting
for the postman.

Tinky the puppy loves to run.

Ben loves a tennis ball to play with,
while another dog prefers a football.

Working gun dog on Exmoor.

Left: Gun dog at work collecting the shot Pheasants.

The Springer Spaniel couldn't resist collecting a dead
oiled razorbill from the beach at Lyme Regis, and the
terrier catches a trout from her owner's trout farm.

Monty the Lurcher sits under
the waterfall on Exmoor.

Soaking wet, a gun dog in training retrieves,
while two dogs play the game of share and
share alike with a stick on the beach.

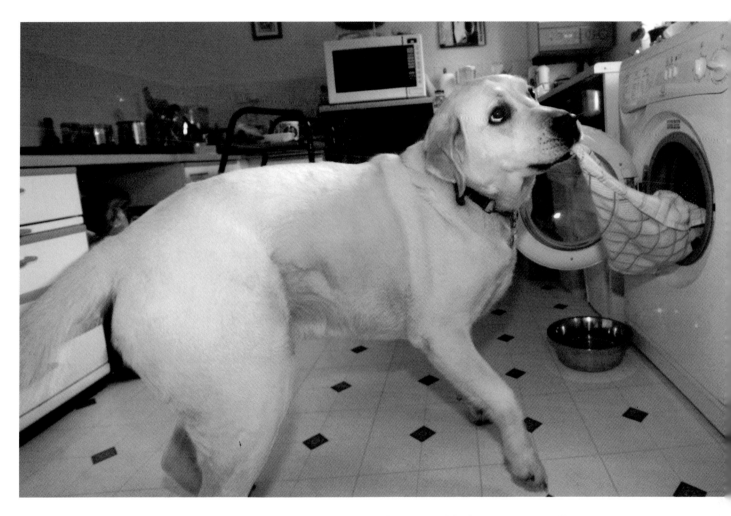

Lee, the Assistance Dog, helping out her disabled owner with the washing, is all in a day's work for the specially trained Labrador.

One mouthful from Great Dane Shannon and
Megan the terrier would be gone, but thankfully
the unusual duo are inseparable
and play all day together.

Biggles the paralysed dog doesn't tolerate other dogs on the beach and sees off
all-comers in his special trolley known locally as the Chariot of Fur.

Biggles splashes through the water in his special trolley.

Chimba the terrier has to spend the rest of her days in her special cradle
after a tragic farming accident left her back legs paralysed.

Right: The Labrador pup plays in the flowers at his Dartmoor home.

Puppies galore all looking for a good home
after being orphaned in Devon.

Right: Tod, flying the flag for his Queen
and country at the Golden Jubilee.

The African Grey Parrot and the Dachshund have a delicate relationship,
hence the peck marks on the dogs nose.

The tiny Yorkshire terrier waits for her master's return at the front door.

It's cold on Exmoor during the winter months, so a winter warmer
from an old sock keeps the puppy called Izzy warm.

Daisy the British Bulldog gets in the mood for the World Cup at Lyme Regis, whilst the Basset Hound keeps his tee shirt on.

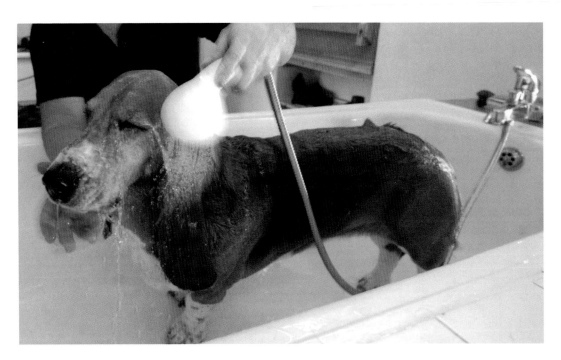

Batty the Basset Hound is
pampered at the Holne
Chase Hotel on Dartmoor.

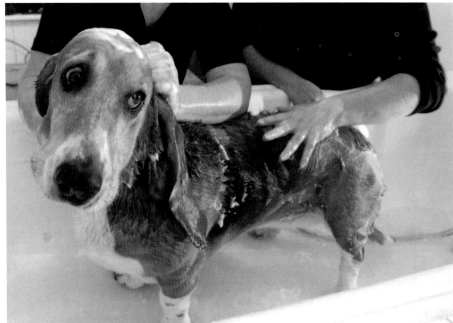

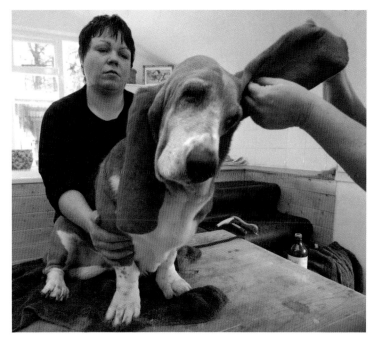

Ollie the King Charles Spaniel plays in a box outside Exeter Magistrates' Court.

All dogs have to be kept clean and well groomed at the RSCPA, including a daily shower and clean teeth.

Boxer dogs pull some pitiful expressions, especially
when it's time to play pool.

Brandy the famous dog from the Nags Head pub in Lyme Regis thinks he's in the driver's seat.